LAKE DISTRICT
Towns & Villages

JOHN WATNEY

The scenery of the Lake District still inspires visitors from all over the world, as it did Wordsworth and the other Lake poets; but equally attractive in their different ways are the towns and villages. The towns are full of interesting buildings, museums and historical associations. Keswick, with its 13th-century charter, is the oldest town in the National Park and is much admired for its lakeside setting at the foot of high fells, while the twin towns of Bowness and Windermere are reminiscent of Victorian seaside resorts. Many of the farming villages date from the 17th century and, with their charming buildings built from the local stone, they offer retreats from the crowds as well as bases for fell and lakeside walks.

KENDAL

The old town of Kendal, known as the Gateway to the Southern Lakes, is famous among walkers and climbers for its mint cake – the quick-energy confection carried in their backpacks. In the Middle Ages, almost its entire population was engaged in the wool industry, particularly a cloth known as 'Kendal green', which was mentioned by Shakespeare in his play *Henry IV, Part I*. Its industries today are shoes, snuff and chewing-tobacco. Its houses, some part-timbered, are grouped around courtyards known as 'yards' with narrow entrances which, with 'The Shambles', make for pleasant browsing. The town is overlooked by the ruins of the 12th-century castle where Catherine Parr, the sixth wife of Henry VIII, was born.

To gain an understanding of Kendal's history, visit the Museum of Lakeland Life and Industry at Abbot Hall. Here farmhouse rooms, workshops and shops of different periods have been recreated with great realism, and there is an abundance of tools, gadgets and everyday artefacts. The Museum of Natural History and Archaeology, near the railway station, has a series of dioramas depicting the geology and natural history of southern Lakeland. Opposite Nether Bridge, the last downstream bridge over the River Kent in the town, is Romney House, where the portrait artist George Romney lived, and died in 1802. It is open to the public in so far as it is now a bed-and-breakfast house. There is a good collection of George Romney's work in the Abbot Hall Art Gallery.

RIGHT
The 13th-century Church of the Holy and Undivided Trinity is the widest parish church in England. It has five aisles in a width of 103ft (32m), and 15 angels look down from the high ceiling.

LEFT
The plaque on the outside of Romney House. Romney was first apprenticed to a cabinetmaker, and married a Cumbrian girl.

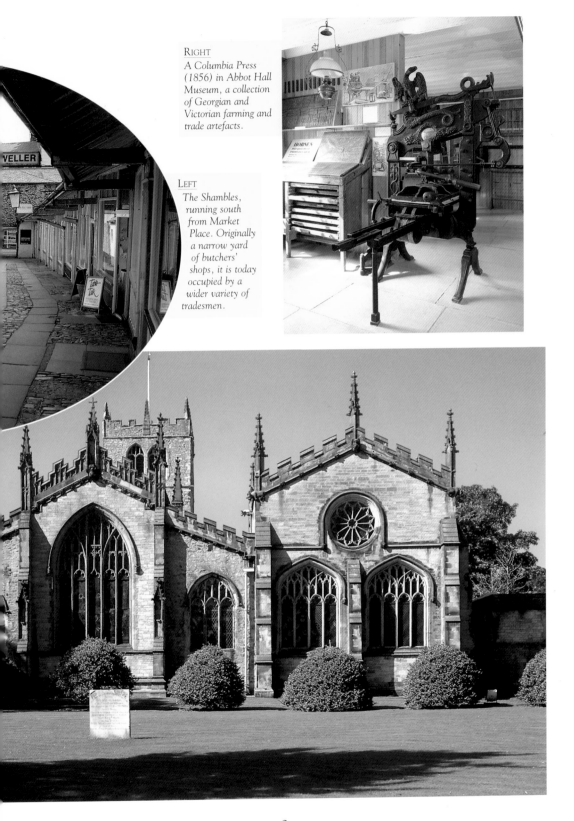

RIGHT
A Columbia Press (1856) in Abbot Hall Museum, a collection of Georgian and Victorian farming and trade artefacts.

LEFT
The Shambles, running south from Market Place. Originally a narrow yard of butchers' shops, it is today occupied by a wider variety of tradesmen.

BOWNESS & WINDERMERE

These two towns run into each other, and are unashamedly tourist-oriented. With their long lakeside frontage and busy steamers, they have the air of a seaside resort. The top visitor attraction is Windermere Lake Cruises, with more than a million passengers a year. Another great draw is the World of Beatrix Potter Exhibition in Bowness. The latest temptation is Windermere Submarine, where you can spend an hour in the murky depths of the lake. Alternatively, visit Lakeside Aquatarium, which offers a 'tour' of the length of a river from mountain to sea.

Bowness grew from a fishing village, while Windermere was built around the railway, which arrived in 1848. The Victorians' grand houses were sited to give fine views, while large hotels provided music and dancing. In both

LEFT
Vintage vessels of the Steam Boat Association of Great Britain meet during a rally at the Windermere Steamboat Museum.

LEFT
Espérance, built in 1869, is the oldest boat on Lloyd's Register of Yachts, and one of the working exhibits at the Windermere Steamboat Museum.

towns, shops, eating places and pubs have taken over the buildings in the centre, but many still proclaim the skill and robustness of their Victorian builders. St Martin's Church, dating from 1483, stands in the oldest and least modernised part of Windermere; its east window bears the coat-of-arms of George Washington's family.

BELOW
Bowness Bay is one of the ports of call of Windermere Lake Cruises, which operate throughout the year.

Windermere Steamboat Museum is a must for classic and steamboat enthusiasts. The Victorian and Edwardian steamboats and launches, all in bandbox condition, lie under cover but afloat and ready to steam. Yet most spent long years submerged in the mud and silt of various lakes. They are the restored relics of the days when the lakes were commercial highways, and the gentry raced their yachts while their families watched and picnicked on little steam launches.

TROUTBECK, WATERHEAD & AMBLESIDE

The village of Troutbeck, with its collection of 17th- and 18th-century farmhouses built around wells, has been declared a Conservation Area. Townend, at the south of the village, was built in 1626 by a yeoman farmer and is now owned by the National Trust. Inside are the original furniture and other possessions of the Browne family, breeders of the hardy Herdwick sheep. Other places of interest are the old village school and the church, with its 1873 east window, in part the work of Edward Burne-Jones.

Waterhead is the lakeside outpost of Ambleside and the northerly port of call for Windermere Lake Cruises; it also has facilities for launching and hiring boats. To the west, cradled in a bend of the River Rothay, are the foundation stones of the Roman fort Galava which, for 300 years from about AD 100, housed some 500 auxiliaries. Keen gardeners will be delayed on their way into Ambleside by Hayes Garden World. The result of four generations of gardening expertise, it is as much a horticultural exhibition as a market, and draws a million customers and visitors a year.

Ambleside is a medieval village enlarged by the Victorians, and in summer has a town-sized population. It is ideally placed for Windermere, Rydal, Grasmere and the Langdale Pikes. Apart from its crowd of shops, it has no less than 66 listed buildings, the one most quickly recognised being the tiny 17th-century Bridge House spanning the Rothay.

LEFT
At the northern end of Windermere, the cruise boats call in at Waterhead, near Ambleside.

BELOW
*Strung out along a hillside lane, Troutbeck is
a charming and unspoilt little village of local
stone and whitewashed houses. It has an
old-world pub but no shop.*

ABOVE
*The Old Mill on North Road
in Ambleside boasts a fine
reproduction waterwheel.*

RIGHT
*Built as a summer house,
the quaint Bridge House in
the heart of Ambleside now
houses a National Trust
information office.*

GRASMERE

The rough grey-slate village, lying in a wooded vale surrounded by craggy mountains, is always thronged with visitors. Those who feel overwhelmed can find refuge in a delightful walk beside the River Rothay, suitable for wheelchairs and with benches for the weary. In Grasmere, every stone evokes memories of William Wordsworth and the other Lake poets, Samuel Taylor Coleridge and Robert Southey. Beside the square-towered church of St Oswald, in 'God's Acre', are Wordsworth's simple grave and Coleridge's more elaborate headstone.

The annual rush-bearing ceremony takes place on the Saturday nearest to St Oswald's Day, 5 August, and every participating child gets a piece of Grasmere gingerbread, which has been made and sold in a cottage beside the lych gate since 1854. Grasmere is also a centre for traditional Lakeland sports.

BELOW
The view across Grasmere to the village of the same name would have been familiar to Wordsworth and his friends.

ABOVE
The cottage by the lych gate, which was the village school from 1685 to 1854, became famous as Sarah Nelson's gingerbread shop, still open today.

LEFT
Local children taking part in Grasmere's famous rush-bearing ceremony held each summer.

WILLIAM WORDSWORTH

At the south end of Grasmere village is Dove Cottage. Formerly a rustic pub, it was here that Wordsworth lived from 1799 to 1808, and where he brought his bride, Mary Hutchinson, in 1802. The poet used to work in the summerhouse overlooking the fellside garden he designed with his sister Dorothy. He left it with regret because of his growing family, and moved to nearby Rydal Mount, an 18th-century enlargement of an older farmhouse, where he spent 37 years. From his bedroom window, Wordsworth looked out to the modest Rydal Water, a joy for skaters in the days when it froze over in winter. In St Mary's Church in Rydal, his pew is at the left front, and behind the church is Dora's Field.

ABOVE
Dove Cottage is now run by the Wordsworth Trust and is visited by students and admirers of the poet from all over the world.

ABOVE LEFT
A tinted pencil drawing of Wordsworth by Henry Edridge ARA, made in 1806 when the poet was living at Dove Cottage.

BELOW
In the summer months, Rydal Mount is open for visitors to see the original layout of the gardens as well as family portraits and possessions inside the house.

INSET BELOW
Dora's Field is a sloping patch of land, bought by Wordsworth in 1826 for his daughter. The field is still 'a host of golden daffodils' every spring.

HAWKSHEAD

A century ago, Hawkshead, east of Coniston, was described as 'the quaintest and most old-world village imaginable'. Despite the pressures of tourism and the inevitable tidying-up improvements, it is still in part extremely picturesque. The old Grammar School – with the desk at which Wordsworth learned his lessons between 1779 and 1787, and on which he carved his name – and Ann Tyson's Cottage, where he lodged, draw fans from far and wide. Ann and her lodger later moved to Colthouse, a hamlet a mile to the east where the 1688 Friends Meeting House remains in good condition. Hawkshead's 15th-century courthouse, once a medieval manor house, is now a National Trust museum of rural life.

LEFT
Today Ann Tyson's cottage is a guest house which otherwise is not open to the public, but a plaque on the wall identifies it with Wordsworth.

BELOW
Hawkshead Courthouse is now owned by the National Trust and contains exhibitions about local crafts and industry.

BELOW
The old Grammar School, formerly attended by Wordsworth, is open to the public in the summer, and houses an exhibition room and a library.

BEATRIX POTTER

Esthwaite Water, a sylvan lakelet, lies between Hawkshead and the twin villages of Near Sawrey and Far Sawrey, a neighbourhood of good houses in good grounds. In Near Sawrey is Hill Top, the 17th-century farmhouse with cottage garden where Beatrix Potter lived and wrote many of her delightful children's books featuring Peter Rabbit, Mrs Tiggy-winkle, Squirrel Nutkin and many other characters. It contains her furniture, china and some of her original drawings, but it is very small, and the National Trust, who own it, restrict visitors to 800 a day. The National Trust also own the former office of William Heelis, Beatrix Potter's solicitor husband, in Hawkshead. Inside it is substantially unchanged, but is now run as a gallery of the author's original drawings for her books.

ABOVE
Beatrix Potter photographed outside Hill Top. Born in London in 1866, she later moved to Lakeland from where she published her first book in 1902.

ABOVE
Hill Top, Beatrix Potter's farm-house home where she wrote and illustrated her children's books, is now a museum.

RIGHT
Peter Rabbit, one of Beatrix Potter's most popular children's characters.

Windermere, viewed from the north, with Waterhead on the left, makes the perfect setting for a summer boat trip.

CONISTON

The village of Coniston, with its streets of substantial stone-built shops beside older whitewashed cottages, clings to the rugged escarpment of Old Man; the name is a corruption of the Gaelic Alt Maen, or High Rock. Old Man is pockmarked by old copper workings, the area's industry before tourism, which arrived with the railway in the 19th century.

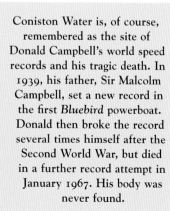

In 1859, the high noon of railway travel, the Furness Railway Company placed a comfortable steam yacht, the *Gondola*, on Coniston Water to take visitors up and down the lake in summer. The yacht remained in service until 1937 when she became first a houseboat and then a beached wreck. In 1977, the National Trust began restoring her to her original high Victorian elegance, and in the summer of 1980 she again steamed on Coniston Water. The National Trust do not exaggerate when they say passengers can travel on her in opulent style. She makes a pleasant way to reach Brantwood, the home of John Ruskin; an alternative is to take the 1920s launch from Coniston Boating Centre, which is also a public launching site.

BELOW
Donald Campbell (left) in the cockpit of Bluebird on Coniston, just before his last and fatal attempt to improve his speed record.

Coniston Water is, of course, remembered as the site of Donald Campbell's world speed records and his tragic death. In 1939, his father, Sir Malcolm Campbell, set a new record in the first *Bluebird* powerboat. Donald then broke the record several times himself after the Second World War, but died in a further record attempt in January 1967. His body was never found.

John Ruskin

The 19th-century art critic and social reformer, John Ruskin, described the Vale of Yewdale, through which one approaches Coniston from Ambleside, as 'the most beautiful valley in England'. In Coniston, the Ruskin Museum tells of his life and philosophy. Ruskin is buried in the churchyard beneath a fine runic cross carved with figures symbolic of his writing. His home from 1872 until his death in 1900 was Brantwood, on the east side of the lake, now filled with his drawings and watercolours. There are frequent alternating displays of his works and themes in the house, with exhibitions of contemporary arts and crafts and theatrical events during the summer.

LEFT
John Ruskin (1819–1900) photographed at Brantwood. He helped to establish the Pre-Raphaelites, and pronounced on many social and educational matters. Ruskin College, Oxford, is named after him.

BELOW
Brantwood, on the eastern side of the lake, commands superb lake and mountain views from its elevated position.

Newby Bridge & Lakeside

At one time, Furness Railway ran a branch line from Ulverston to Newby Bridge and Lakeside to meet the Windermere steamboats. Today only a three-and-a-half-mile section from Haverthwaite remains, but it still does the same job with its standard-gauge steam trains meeting the lake steamers – a delightful way to travel to the area south of Windermere. The oldest of the three steamers on the lake is *Tern*, dating from 1891.

The Newby Bridge dates from the 16th century, and the village has an 18th-century inn which accommodates tourists visiting the nearby bobbin mill and Fell Foot Country Park, which caters for all forms of non-powered boating.

RIGHT
The Victorian Stott Park bobbin mill, still working in steam, is a popular attraction.

BELOW
Steam boats link up with steam trains at Lakeside at the southern end of Windermere.

ABOVE
The five-arched bridge, from which Newby Bridge takes its name, spans the River Leven as it flows from Windermere to Morecambe Bay.

AROUND ESKDALE

Near the vertiginous Hardknott Pass, with its view to the sea from the summit, is Boot, a huddle of white-washed cottages. Beyond an ancient stone bridge over Whillan Beck, a watermill has been working since 1578. Vestiges of Nab Gill iron mines, closed in 1882, are marked by great pink stains down the fellside, spillage of haematite from the gravity-powered wagons that brought it from the top. At its foot are the clearly defined remains of Boot's station platform, loading bays and office. The Ravenglass and

ABOVE
The steam trains of the Ravenglass and Eskdale Railway run from Ravenglass via Muncaster mill to this terminus at Dalegarth, near Boot.

BELOW
Muncaster Castle, home of the Pennington family since the 13th century, is open to the public, as are its gardens which are famed for their rhododendrons and azaleas.

The world-famous Lake District Owl Conservation Trust, set in the grounds of Muncaster Castle, is the headquarters of the World Owl Trust, which works for owl conservation on an international scale.

Eskdale Railway, better known as 'La'al Ratty', now runs steam trains the seven miles from nearby Dalegarth to Ravenglass.

Ravenglass stands by a tidal lagoon from which the sea is out of sight for hours a day. The coast here has changed enormously in the 2,000 years since it was the Roman fort of Glannoventa. All that remains now is a bath house tucked in a wood, one of the tallest Roman buildings extant in England.

Nearby Muncaster Castle has history, treasures, a famous 77-acre garden, and an Owl Centre. A short way off is Muncaster Watermill which has been producing flour since 1455. Here, one can see the 19th-century wooden machinery working, watch the miller at work, taste his wife's scones and bran cake, and buy stone-ground organic flour.

ABOVE
The village of Boot, seen from the Nab Gill iron mines' fellside wagonway, with its derelict railway terminus in the foreground.

BUTTERMERE

The road round Crummock Water goes to Buttermere village – no more than a church, two inns and some farms, surrounded by steep mountain scenery. The Fish Hotel was once the home of Mary Robinson, the 'Beauty of Buttermere', who was conned into marriage by a forger, James Hatfield, in 1802. Operating in Keswick, he presented himself as the Honourable Augustus Hope, and hobnobbed with the gentry. Mary was widowed when he was hanged in Carlisle. Later she had a happy marriage to a farmer, and was eventually buried in Caldbeck churchyard. A path from Buttermere leads to Scale Force, the highest waterfall in Cumbria.

BELOW
The daughter of the landlord of the Fish Hotel became the 'Beauty of Buttermere'. It is one of the two pubs heavily patronised by fell walkers.

ABOVE
Buttermere lies in a lovely valley deep in the Cumbrian Mountains.

INSET ABOVE
The gate of the church porch depicts a shepherd with his flock on the hillside.

Cockermouth lies only five fields outside the National Park and is overlooked by its high fells. Its Main Street is a boulevard, which gives the town a continental air, and along it is an astonishing number of sites to visit. The William Creighton Mineral Museum is an Aladdin's Cave of strange and colourful rocks, crystals and semi-precious stones. Next door is the Georgian house where Wordsworth was born on 7 July 1770, and his sister Dorothy on Christmas Day 1771. The Working Museum of Printing is behind a 16th-century shop. The Toy and Model Museum is filled with thousands of toys dating back to 1900, with a superb model railway and car racing circuit. Aspects of Motoring, in the old maltings of Jennings Brewery, has over 300 cars spanning nearly a century, every one in running order. Jennings, which supplies 100 pubs in Cumbria, offers tours of its brewery. The town also has an art gallery, Castlegate, opposite the 14th-century castle. Fletcher Christian, leader of the mutiny on the *Bounty*, was born here in Moorland Close in 1764.

THE CUMBERLAND TOY & MODEL MUSEUM

ABOVE
The sheep market at Cockermouth takes place weekly.

LEFT
There are many visitor-operated displays at the Cumberland Toy and Model Museum, including a helicopter.

BELOW
This fine Georgian house was built in 1745 for the Sheriff of Cumberland. It was later owned by the 1st Earl of Lonsdale, who let it to his Estate and Law Agent, John Wordsworth. Here all five of his children were born, including the Poet Laureate.

AROUND BORROWDALE

At the foot of Honister Pass lies Seatoller, a village built in 1643 for the slate quarries at the summit of the pass. The Lake District Park Dalehead Base in the village houses displays on the geology and history of the area. Further north in the beautiful valley of Borrowdale, Castle Crag, a rocky tree-clad pyramid, forms a dramatic background to the tiny hamlet of Grange. A pretty cluster of white-painted cottages, it is mentioned in Hugh Walpole's *The Herries Chronicle*. Watendlath is a popular destination for walkers, and, unfortunately, motorists. As the narrow, twisting approach road is totally unsuited to the heavy summer traffic, a more environmentally gentle method of transport is the free National Trust Wanderer minibus that runs from Keswick on Sundays.

TOP
Watendlath is a cluster of five farmhouses in a hanging valley, with a tiny tarn.

ABOVE
Seatoller is a good base for nature walks and exploration around Honister Pass.

LEFT
Grange, a picture postcard village, is reached by an ancient stone bridge spanning the River Derwent.

⤙ · KESWICK · ⤚

The town of Keswick is bordered on three sides by high mountains, while the fourth opens onto the island-studded Derwentwater, beyond which are the Jaws of Borrowdale and, more distant, Scafell Pike. Its oldest monument, half a mile east of the town, is Castlerigg Stone Circle – 60 rough-hewn stones dated about 1400 BC. The town's centrepiece is the church-like Moot Hall with a one-handed clock on its tower, below which is the Tourist Information Centre. Greta Hall, built in 1800, is the former home of both Samuel Taylor Coleridge and poet laureate Robert Southey.

Next door is Keswick's most popular visitor attraction, the Cumberland Pencil Works. In the 1500s, graphite was mined in nearby Borrowdale, and pencil-making was a cottage industry; today the graphite is imported and the pencils mass-produced. The Pencil Museum in the works has a replica of a Seathwaite graphite mine, and a video showing pencil-making.

Keswick Museum and Gallery, built in 1897, exhibits an instructive scale model of the Lake District, a fine collection of minerals, and works by Southey and Sir Hugh Walpole. In the churchyard at St Kentigern's parish church at Crosthwaite are the graves of 16 famous names of the 18th and 19th centuries, and several generations of the Southey family. Inside the church is a splendid white marble recumbent figure of Southey. A new theatre is currently being built on the lake shore. From Manor Park, passenger launches call at six places around the lake.

ABOVE
The 1813 Moot Hall is the focal point of the town centre. In 1276 Edward I granted Keswick a market charter, and a market is still held here every Saturday.

RIGHT
At the south end of the town, rowing boats can be hired on Derwentwater, and a launch service takes walkers and trippers to various points around the lake.

LEFT
A stunning
view of
Derwentwater
from Friar's Crag,
near Keswick, with
Causey Pike beyond.

ABOVE
Ashness Bridge, on the tortuous road
from Keswick to Watendlath, is probably
the most photographed site in the Lake
District with its panoramic view over
Derwentwater and the Skiddaw massif.

CALDBECK

Caldbeck is the northernmost village within the National Park, and also one of the most interesting. Of immediate note is John Peel's large, ornate gravestone in the graveyard of 12th-century St Kentigern's Church, with its holy well used for baptisms. There is a mill with moving wheel, a goldsmith, a clog-maker, an 1810 brewery building, and Oddfellows, the last remaining of 17 public houses in mid-19th-century Caldbeck when it was a mining village. Most impressive, though rarely seen by visitors, is 'The Howk', a limestone gorge with waterfalls and cauldrons astride which stand the ruins of a large 1857 bobbin mill which had the largest waterwheel in England – it was melted down for the war effort in 1940.

ABOVE
The remains of a 19th-century bobbin mill in The Howk are almost overwhelmed by trees and undergrowth.

LEFT
A colourful corner of the award-winning village of Caldbeck.

BELOW AND INSET RIGHT
At St Kentigern's Church is the gravestone of John Peel, the famous huntsman, and his family.

IN MEMORY OF
JOHN PEEL OF
RUTHWAITE who died
Nov 13ᵗʰ 1854 aged 78 Years.
Also MARY his wife who
died Aug 9ᵗʰ 1859 aged 82.
Also JONATHAN their Son
who died Jan 21ˢᵗ 1806.
aged 9 Years.
Also PETER their Son who
died Nov 15ᵗʰ 1840.
aged 27 Years.
Also MARY DAVIDSON their
DAUGHTER who died Nov 30
1863, aged 42 years.
Also JOHN their Son who died
Nov 22 1821 aged 50 Years.

AROUND ULLSWATER

Glenridding, once a mining village, is now a tourist centre for steamer cruises on Ullswater and for fell walking. Patterdale has a parish church dedicated to St Patrick who, it is claimed, walked here after being shipwrecked on Duddon Sands. Dacre is a sleepy place with a storybook castle and an interesting Norman church, in the churchyard of which are four mysterious carved stones. They show a bear asleep, being attacked by a cat, fighting the cat, and then eating it. Pooley Bridge provides a base for walking the hills around Ullswater. Lake cruises are the most popular activity, and from the pier steamers ply to Howtown and Glenridding seven miles south. Ullswater is a public highway, but there are speed restrictions and other regulations.

RIGHT
Pleasure boats steam the length of Ullswater from Glenridding to Pooley Bridge via Howtown. Ullswater is said to be reminiscent of the Swiss lakes.

ABOVE
One of the strange stone bear carvings in the churchyard at Dacre.

LEFT
Dacre Castle, a 14th-century pele tower, is well preserved and open to the public by appointment.